Cat Training

Basics

Beginner's Guide to Raising and Training Your Cat So
That It Behaves the Way You Want While Also
Unlearning Some of Its Bad Habits

By Manuel Hollis

Contents

Thank you for buying this book and I hope that you will find it useful. If you will want to share your thoughts on this book, you can do so by leaving a review on the Amazon page, it helps me out a lot.

Chapter 1: Basic Training For Your Cat

Cats are animals. People are animals too; but apparently of a higher order. So as to cohabit in a delighted relationship, there are several things that your cat has to find out. Having an animal of any kind ought to be enjoyable, however, there is going to be substantial pain in case the animal is in control of the home. So what are the basics of the training which your cat has to develop?

Initially, there is toilet training. There would be absolutely nothing worse than arriving home from a difficult day at the workplace to discover an immense mess on your finest piece of furniture. So where to go to the toilet is among the essential things to demonstrate to your cat or kitty. Cats are usually tidy animals, so it is rather simple to train it to utilize a litter tray. Just put the cat on it after the meal.

Training also might depend upon where you reside. If you reside in an apartment, you might have to teach your cat to lead so that you could take it outside. If you reside in the countryside, this might not be needed. If you live near huge traffic yet have a yard, you might have to teach your cat to stay clear of the roadway, or otherwise, the cat is very likely to get run over.

Another essential thing that is going to require attention is stopping the cat from scratching the furnishings. Cats like to scratch, and it is natural for them to hone their claws. They do not simply do it to mess up furnishings, however, this is what is going to occur when they are not taught. Take away the cat from the furnishings the instant it begins to scratch and position its paws versus the scratching pole.

In case you travel a great deal and want to take your cat with you, travel training is a necessity. It's not a good idea to give your cat the liberty in the automobile, as it might climb on you as you are driving, and this may result in an accident. Additionally, in case you have an accident with the cat loose in the automobile, it may be hurt needlessly. A cat travel cage ought to be utilized. However, ensure it is steadied by utilizing a safety belt to hold it in place.

It is also vital to teach your cat not to climb up the windows and screen doors. To spare your screen, set up a cat door and teach the cat on how to go through it. The majority of people begin with a kitty instead of a mature cat, so it is simpler to train them. When cats have grown completely, it is extremely difficult to break some of their naughty habits, so begin when they are young and keep at it. Do not allow them to get away with habits that are not acceptable.

Chapter 2: Gaining Your Cat's Respect

Whenever people choose to have a pet, there are certain guidelines that ought to be set up. Keep in mind that your place is not your pet's natural territory and that all animals still act as animals regardless of where they are. Attempting to alter your cat's bad habits needs consistency and persistence. In case you like your cat, the final thing you desire is to appear as the opponent - somebody to be disliked and perhaps feared.

So how to teach your cat so that its habits are acceptable in your world while still remaining buddies? The solution is not to let the cat rule the roost. Your cat is not going to respect you while it is in charge.

You have to let the cat understand who is the boss while still getting its trust and love. This implies that the cat needs to be awarded favorably with snacks and snuggles when it does something that you approve of. However, when the cat wants to do things he understands you do not like, you need to stay calm, while being just as insistent to get your way. From the time when they are kitties, cats are going to follow the authority of the queen cat, their mom. So you need to take on that position in the cat's life.

One method to accomplish this is to bring the kitty around by the scruff of the neck sometimes. This is the manner in which the mom would have moved the kitty. The scruff is the baggy skin on the rear of the neck. It is rather simple to get, and both kitties and grown cats can be carried around like this without pain. You are going to see that when you pick the cat up like this, it is going to, all of a sudden, go limp and simply hang there. That is precisely what the cat would do if the mom had the kitten in her mouth by the scruff. Even when your cat is no more a kitty, it is going to let you bring it by the scruff without grievance. So when you see the cat doing things it should not do, pick it up by the scruff and place it down far from the mischief.

Make certain your cat has lots of stimulation and play so that it is not bored, which is going boost the chances of it being a more polite cat, too. Squeaky and soft toys are going to keep the cat's attention concentrated on play rather than mischief. Even a big paper bag or a cardboard box can captivate the cat for hours.

Chapter 3: Litterbox Training Your Cat

Among the essential things to do with your brand-new cat or kitty is training it to utilize the litter box. In the wild, among the cat's better actions is to scratch a hole in something soft to go to the toilet. This action is still prevalent in domesticated ones, and that makes it simpler to teach them. When cats can access a backyard - specifically one with a garden, they are going to choose to go out frequently. However, if your cat is restricted to your property or apartment, it is vital to give it a box or litter tray to protect against puddles and other unpleasant things.

The litter tray ought to be broad and shallow while having vertical sides. This is going to assist in maintaining the medium as the cat is digging and scratching. It ought to remain in a location where human traffic is at a minimum. The laundry is typically the location selected for the litter tray. Sand could be utilized in the tray, however, commercial cat-litter is finest because of its high absorbency. And cats appear to like utilizing it.

In case you have a brand-new kitty, it is not untimely to begin training it to utilize the litter box right away. As quickly as the cat has actually wrapped up drinking its milk, take it to the litter tray and set it down carefully on the litter. It's an excellent idea to feed the cat near the litter tray in the beginning, so that it understands where it is. In case you feed your brand-new kitty in the kitchen area, and after that, bring it into the laundry to the litter tray, you can't expect it to know its way to the laundry the following time.

So feed the kitty beside the litter tray up until the routine of using it is well developed. After this, it is going to be feasible to alter the feeding location if that is necessary. In case the kitty creates a puddle anyplace other than in the litter tray, make certain to clean it up with powerful-smelling disinfectant to totally get rid of the smell, or or else, the cat is just going to follow its nose the following time it has to go.

When you have put the kitty onto the litter tray a couple of times, it is going to understand what it needs to do quickly. Cats and kitties are really simple to train to utilize a litter tray. Positioning an appealing cover across the litter tray is a great idea, however, make certain the cat understands how to utilize the tray without the cover initially. Then you may cover it up and demonstrate to the cat how to get it.

Chapter 4: Which Cat Behaviors Should You Break?

There are numerous behaviors that are not appropriate for pets. Nevertheless, much is going to depend upon your own lifestyleand whether you reside in the nation or the city. Among the worst cat behaviors is scratching, especially when it comes to scratching people. Cats' claws could cause fairly bad scratches, so this is one habit that ought to be dissuaded as much as feasible. It is not going to be attainable to remove it completely as it is the cat's nature to scratch, and it does it to defend itself. Making certain your cat is not scared and never ever feels endangered is going to go a long way in protecting against scratching you or loved ones.

Spraying is additional behavior that is unwanted in the house. Cats spray to tag their area, so it is just a natural thing for them. One method to dissuade this is to purchase a pheromone bottle. It is an artificial cat spray and is odor-free to people, however, cats can smell it. In case your cat believes another cat has actually defined its territory, then it will not be so likely to do the identical thing.

Leaping onto high locations is additionally typical cat conduct, however, it might not fit in with your way of life in case you have antique vases resting on racks. Neither is it healthy to have a cat on the counter as you are prepping food for the kids. Cats could be a risk to themselves and others when they leap suddenly onto locations that might not support them.

It goes without stating that you are going to wish your cat to utilize the litter tray. In case it does not, it might need to turn into an outdoor cat. One more behavior that is natural for cats is hunting. We want them to capture rats and mice, however, when the cat comes in licking feathers from its jowls, you never know if that little bird was among those dealing with extinction. A bell on its collar is going to assist in stopping the cat from killing a lot of birds.

It's not a good thing to be snuggled up to cat just to have it suddenly sink its teeth into your arm. Yet biting is additionally a natural cat behavior. In case your cat is a biter, dissuade it by positioning it on the floor right away when it bites. It might be that the cat had actually finished with snuggling, and this was its method of letting you understand. If the biting appears extreme, you might have to have that newspaper ready. The cat is quickly going to learn not to bite.

Chapter 5: Stopping Scratching and Clawing

There is absolutely nothing worse than a cat which is continuously scratching the furnishings. Your gorgeous furniture could be messed up extremely fast by this behavior, so it is a good idea to find a solution for it as quickly as you can.

Scratching is a cat's natural behavior, so it is not going to be feasible to stop it from doing it completely. What you need to do is teach it to scratch on a thing that does not matter. Scratching poles crafted from rope wound around a rod are created specifically for this function. It is a great plan to obtain one as quickly as you get your kitty. In case you teach the kitty to utilize it right from when it is small, then it is going to be a lot simpler.

If the cat does not appear to enjoy the scratching pole as much as your finest chair, then purchase a bit catmint and place it on the rope. The scent is extremely appealing to cats. Additionally, get a spray bottle loaded with water to spray in the cat's face when it scratches your furnishings. Cats dislike water on their faces. There is just one issue with this; your furnishings might be French-polished, and therefore, watermark really easily.

The idea is to train a cat, not harm it, so roll up a couple of sheets of newspaper and utilize it to tap the cat's face. It is not going to harm the cat, however, the cat is going to dislike the sound and feel of it. This is additionally an excellent way to stop the cat from scratching individuals. After being smacked with it a couple of times, merely hearing the rustle of paper is going to stop the cat typically. In some cases, cats are going to crouch around a corner and spring out at you or the kids. Do not forget that although it is regular conduct for a cat to do this kind of thing, it has to be managed, or it might result in harm.

The rolled-up paper technique is going to dissuade the cat from scratching and pouncing quickly. In case you hold the cat up by the scruff of the neck simultaneously, you are going to signal dominance over the cat, informing it you are the top cat. Smack the cat gently on the face or paws with the paper, and after that, put the cat down. In case your cat puts out its claws when you are cuddling it, carefully push at them up until it withdraws them. By doing this, you are going to teach the cat that having claws out while being cuddled is inappropriate conduct.

Chapter 6: How to Protect Your Houseplants From Cats

Lots of folks grow beautiful houseplants that contribute to the atmosphere of their house. However, what takes place when cat attacks and consumes the houseplant you were so happy with? One day you have a nice-looking plant, the following day, the only thing left to do is toss it in the garbage can. Naughty cat! However, wait prior to spanking.

Initially, you ought to determine what induced your cat to strike the plant. There are 2 primary reasons why cats eat plants. One reason is that green food is part of their eating plan. If your cat has actually not been provided with any veggies or plants to eat, it might be merely following its survival instinct. In this particular case, make certain that the cat gets to go out regularly so it can eat the grasses of its very own selection. Consuming grass is going to additionally assist in eliminating fur balls that can stick in its throat. In case you can not let your cat outdoors, then grow some particular cat grass in a pot and permit the cat access to it. An excellent pet store is going to offer the appropriate type of seed.

Additional reason why the cat might have assaulted the plant is that the breeze moved its leaves; therefore, it ended up being an opponent to be assaulted and eaten. This is natural conduct for cats in the wilderness. If this holds true, then move the plant to a location where the cat can not easily see it-- someplace far from breezes and drafts. It might be enough to put the plant upon a low table, or you might require a higher rack for it.

Obviously, as soon as the cat has actually had a fantastic time damaging that plant you enjoyed so much, he may choose he wishes to do it constantly. In this instance, you might need to live without indoor plants or keep the cat restricted to an area where there are none when you are out of your home. However, it might have been pure boredom that made the cat strike the plant-- the cat might have simply required something or somebody to play with. Provide the cat with lots of attention when you are home. Ensure it has lots of its own toys. They don't have to be pricey toys; homemade toys are simple to make and quickly replenishable.

Dangle a little wisp of scrunched up paper a couple of inches off the flooring by tying it from something with string. A chair rung will do, or a cabinet doorknob. The cat is going to like pouncing on this and wrestling on its rear with it. A light, little ball is going to have the cat skittering over the floor as it chases it. With a lot else to interest the cat, it ought to quickly forget about the plants.

Chapter 7: How to Make Sure Your Cat Doesn't Get on Counters and Tables.

One essential thing in teaching your cat is to stop it from leaping up on the counter or table. You might believe its not a problem to have a cat on the counter-- as a matter of fact, some individuals might think that it is rather charming. However, stop and think about it. Cat does not truly understand what it is going to land on when it makes that huge jump from flooring to counter. Do you actually want it to land on those cookies that are simply prepared to enter into the oven? Or it might quickly knock something breakable or hot onto the ground. So, what to do?

The secret is to utilize something the cat dislikes to dissuade this behavior. A lot of cats dislike abrupt, loud noise, so in case you make a loud noise in its face when it leaps up, it'll rapidly leap back down. Quickly it'll start to link the noise with that specific activity, and it'll cease. So what can you utilize to produce a loud noise? An empty can of soda with a couple of marbles or pebbles in it is one great idea. Shake it in the cat's face, so it rattles loudly and shocks the cat. The cat is not going to enjoy that. If you additionally say no numerous times really loudly, it might quickly stop hopping as quickly as it hears that command. Some individuals think growling is a great idea. This is how the cat's mom would teach the kitty what is permitted and what isn't. This is one manner in which cats interact with each other, as well.

A bottle loaded with pebbles might additionally be utilized, however, the noise is a little silenced by the plastic. Another idea is to roll a couple of sheets of paper up and slap the counter just before the cat with it. Then, in case it does not leap down, pick him it by the scruff and put it on the floor. Never ever scoop the cat up from the table and kiss or cuddle it, since this is positive reinforcement and is going to motivate it to leap up the following time it desires a bit of attention.

Spraying a cat with a spray bottle filled with tidy water is another approach of dissuading the behavior of leaping onto the counter. If the cat merely does not stop leaping, attempt doing numerous things simultaneously. Keep a kid's horn, the kind you could blow into, close-by. As quickly as the cat reaches the top of the counter, blow the horn in its face, spray the cat in the face with the water and tap it on the head with the rolled-up paper. Do it whenever you find the cat up there, and it'll quickly get fed up with all that and quit.

Chapter 8: How to Make Sure That Your Cat Doesn't Go Out of The Door

If you reside in a metropolitan location or anywhere near a significant traffic route, you might have to stop your cat from going out the door whenever you open it. Cats could be quickly scared in traffic, and you do not wish for your pet to meet with a bad mishap. Not only is an accident going to be distressing for your pet, but vet charges also have a tendency to make a big hole in your budget plan. Stopping the kitten from going out the door is not going to be simple, however, it could be handled with patience. It is definitely simpler to teach a little kitty than a grown one whose habits might be fixed.

Whether you have a cat or a kitty, it is going to have to be taught to remain inside unless you permit it to head out. To do this, utilize the cat's natural qualities, working with its nature instead of versus it. We all understand that cats do not like loud, surprising sounds, so each time the door is open and kitten goes that way, be prepared with a loud noise-- but between the door and it. Do not show up behind the cat with it, or you'll simply scare it right out the door.

One great way to teach your kitten is to get the help of another individual to stand outside the door. Then you could open it, and as quickly as your kitty pokes its nose out, have the other individual spray it with a water gun or a spray bottle. Two individuals are going to do even better. One could have the noisemaker; the other could have a spray bottle. This is going to scare your cat back into the room where you could be waiting to calm it and show it what a great cat it is for returning.

To include a lot more to the lesson, you could be certain to call the cat back right before the noise and water spray. If you make your voice noise alarmed, the kitten is going to get the hint quickly, and it is going to teach it that an alarmed voice implies something undesirable will occur. This could be helpful at other times, as well. The cat might be outdoors in the backyard, and you all of a sudden, it will leap across the fence. Calling the cat back in an alarming voice is going to save the cat from getting lost or chased after by a dog or perhaps another cat.

Obviously, constantly keep in mind to utilize positive reinforcement like treats or petting when the cat does the appropriate thing.

Chapter 9: Which Cat Behaviors Have to be Learned?

There are a variety of behaviors that your cat has to learn so that your relationship is going to be a pleased and worry-free one. Having a cat as a pet has numerous benefits, however, these could be out-weighed if the cat is permitted to rule the roost, particularly if its nature is naughty. Particular behaviors have to be learned by your cat for the security of others in your home, as well as to boost the relationship between cat and people.

A crucial thing for the kitten to learn is to utilize the litter tray. Urinating on furnishings or carpet is going to ruin it for life and leave a smell that is difficult to eliminate. It is additionally harmful to have puddles or other things on the floor where young children might be crawling.

A cat or kitty additionally has to learn to come when called. This renders it simpler to get it out of danger if it has actually wandered away, and it additionally makes feeding time more arranged. If you have to head out and the cat needs to be shut in, you want to be able to call it and have it show up in a sensible time-frame, or you are going to be late for work or any place you were headed to.

Cats are nighttime animals. That's why they, all of a sudden, come to life around sundown and wish to go wandering. That's why they sleep so much during the day. This conduct is inconceivable to stop completely, however, you can keep kitty locked within during the night and have fun with it throughout the day. The less sleep the cat gets during the day, the more it is going to sleep during the night.

In case you travel a ton and wish to take the cat, then it is going to have to discover how to travel conveniently in an automobile, and it is essential for it not to stray and get lost when you reach your destination. It would be a great idea for your cat to find out how to lead in a harness, and after that, you can take it out for a walk without stressing that it is going to stray or bump into harm.

Cats additionally have to discover how not to be harmful. It's a cat's nature to hone its claws and to hunt and leap. These habits are not so accepted in the house, so the cat needs to discover where it is permitted to scratch and what it can jump on securely. The cat does not understand that the stove is going to burn it if it leaps onto it, nor does it understand that it may knock down your precious vase if it hops on that rack. These are the kinds of things a cat has to know.

Chapter 10: Teaching Your Cat to Come When Called.

It is necessary to teach your cat to come when called for a range of reasons. You might have to head out unexpectedly, and you do not want to leave your cat outdoors where it might remain in harm of other lurking dogs or cats chasing it. If you have actually taught your cat to come when called, the goal of getting it within is going to be easy. So how to teach a cat to come when called? Among the simplest methods is to utilize its fondness for food.

You do not need to train the cat to know its name. Cats might be called a name, however, this is typically for the ease of the owners, instead of the cat. Kitten does not care what it is called, and it is frequently going to respond to any name, so long as it is stated in the identical intonation. However, back to utilizing food for training. When time comes to feed your kitten, create a loud and particular sound, such as rattling a knife or spoon on the side of the cat food. The cat is going to link that sound with being fed and come extremely rapidly. However, do not leave it at that. You do not wish to need to rattle a spoon whenever you want your cat to come.

While rattling the spoon, call the cat's name repeatedly. Say it loud enough to be heard despite the rattling spoon. Extremely frequently, a high-pitched 'kitty-kitty' is going to suffice. The cat is going to get accustomed to the rattling spoon signifying food, and the noise of your voice is going to be related to the rattling spoon, which means that the cat is going to come when you just call without rattling the spoon.

It is excellent to strengthen this good behavior by providing a reward, so when the cat comes at your call, and you do not mean to feed it, offer it a little treat rather. It could be a food treat, a cuddle while informing it what a great kitten it is, or you might provide it with a toy and have fun with it for a bit. Kittens love to go after a wisp of paper connected to a string, so it doesn't need to be a pricey toy. Cats react to the generosity and play in addition to food.

If your kitten does not come quickly to be fed, lower the quantity of food you provide it. When the cat is truly starving, it is going to come far more quickly. This is when you should rattle the spoon and call loudly.

Chapter 11: Walking Your Cat

It isn't the most common thing to notice a cat being walked with a leash. Typically, it is dogs that have leashes and cats that wander free. Nevertheless, nowadays, with many little animals and birds on the brink of extinction, you might wish to think about teaching your cat or kitty to walk on a leash. This is going to stop the cat from hunting down and eliminating little birds or butterflies. It is going to stop it from climbing trees to take baby birds from their nests. It is going to additionally keep it out of harm, as you are going to be monitoring its location in a responsible way.

Instead of simply utilizing a leash and a collar to walk your cat, consider utilizing a harness. A cat's head is rather little in comparison to the remainder of it, and a collar might be inclined to pull over its head and off. The harness straps ought to surround the body and the neck simply behind the front legs, with 2 more straps to join the circles together, one down the rear of the neck and one through the front legs. You are going to need a clip for the leash too. Light leather or artificial material is excellent for a cat's harness. Do not utilize anything too bulky, or the cat is going to decline it.

It's additionally essential to get your cat accustomed to the feel and look of the leash prior to you taking it for a walk in it. After the cat has actually ended up being used to seeing the leash (you might leave it in its bed), then let it don it for a couple of minutes every day prior to leading it around by the lead. While still inside, yank lightly on the lead whilst calling your cat. When it comes to you, commend the cat, however never ever scold or force it if it does not come, or it'll believe the leash is a penalty.

As you walk your cat with a leash, do not walk the cat as you would a doggy. Doggies like to run quickly and are more than delighted to trot at a good gait next to you when they have learned to lead. Cats are rather distinct. They do not normally walk or run quickly in a straight line. They have a tendency to stop and go, to wander, and to check unusual rustlings in the grass. For your cat to take pleasure in walking outside with you, you need to permit it to do at least a few of these things. Never ever yank the cat along harshly. The cat is going to be very likely to back off extremely rapidly.

Carefully urge it to come with you and applaud it when it moves in the appropriate direction. Hold out snacks for the cat as you call it to come.

Cats additionally feel the heat quickly. Don't expect to opt for a fast run around the block. Keep in mind that the cat has no shoes for protection from the scorching heat or cold snow. Walk your cat on the grass and in the shade whenever possible. Sun is okay if it's not really that hot.

Regard your cat's requirement to rest as you are walking it. It's a good idea to halt and smell the roses yourself. Let your walk remain in a calm and worry-free environment. Your cat is going to likely be scared of skateboarders zooming past or a loud traffic. With these handful of tips, your cat ought to quickly start to enjoy his everyday walk.

Chapter 12: Teaching the Cat to Sit on Command

Some individuals would have us think that it is inconceivable to train a cat anything, however, if it could be trained to come for its supper, then it could be taught other things too. It might need perseverance and consistency, however, the end outcome is going to be worth it. Few cats have actually been trained to sit on command, yet, it is still possible to train your cat this command. Make certain your cat is wide-awake and a bit hungry prior to you beginning to teach it this

Get the cat used to taking edible snacks from your hand, to ensure that it understands when it smells it, that you have a thing in your hand for it. Pick a time when the cat is standing. Approach it with the reward and allow it to smell it in your closed fist. When it has actually smelled your hand, move it over the top of its head. Not high above it, or it may leap to reach it. Simply move your hand over the top of its head, approximately one inch over it. You are going to see that to keep its nose close to the reward, the cat is going to sit. In case the cat doesn't sit, carefully push on its back-- simply before the tail - up until it does.

Obviously, you need to use voice commands additionally. State "Sit" in a firm voice as you move your hand. As quickly as a cat sits, provide it with the reward and commend it. You have to do this a number of times during the day to remind it of what it is about. It's no use doing it one time this week, and after that, forgetting everything about it up until the following week. Cats are not very likely to keep in mind anything such as that for an entire week.

When your cat sits rapidly for its reward, you can attempt doing it without any reward. Utilize your hand movement, however, with absolutely nothing in the hand. When the cat sits, open the hand, and show the cat that there is absolutely nothing there, however, still commend and stroke it for obeying. The following time you do it and the cat complies, have a reward for it, however, slowly wean it off the snacks. You are going to want to make the cat sit at least two times a day for some time before the cat masters it. When the cat is accustomed to sitting without a reward, attempt using the command without the hand movement. In case the cat does not comply, return to utilizing the hand movement with the reward for a bit longer. By doing this, you are going to teach your cat to sit, and it is going to surprise your buddies.

Chapter 13: Training the Cat to Allow Brushing

Cats enjoy being stroked, so it is simple to train your cat to allow brushing. Brushing is going to assist in getting rid of loose hair and stop the cat from getting a fur ball stuck in its throat. It additionally assists in eliminating annoying prickles it might have picked up on its walks outdoors. You are going to have the ability to keep tabs on the cat's health in case you brush it routinely, too.

Pick a time when the cat is feeling a bit drowsy and wishes to huddle on your warm lap. Have the brush ready, so you do not need to interrupt the cat to get it. In case the cat hasn't seen the brush just before, hold it close to its face so it can smell all of it if that's what the cat wants. In this way, the cat is going to comprehend that it is not going to harm it, therefore, it will not be scared of it. In fact, it's a great strategy to rub your hands along the the brush handle so the cat can discover your scent on it. In case the cat is accustomed to you, it is going to be assured that this weird tool is dependable.

When it has actually checked and allowed the brush, start to brush your cat with slow and mild motions. Constantly brush with the lay of the hair, not versus it. In case the kitten attempts to get the brush with its paws to play with it, place it away instantly. You do not want the cat to begin playing whenever it notices the brush. You want for the cat to discover how to be still and allow you to brush it.

As quickly as a kitten has actually quieted down, begin to brush it once again. Begin at approximately ear level and work in reverse with a long, fluid motion. Never ever attempt to brush its face, or you may harm its tender whiskers and eyes. Brushing the tangles out of terribly matted hair can induce pain, so do it carefully. In case the cat anticipates discomfort whenever it sees the brush, it is not going to be open to the process.

Numerous various brushes could be beneficial when grooming your pet. A big brush with stiff bristles is great for the body, while a tinier, softer brush could be better for the tummy and tail. In case your cat has long tail hairs, you might require a brush with bristles which are a bit stiffer. A comb could additionally be a useful component of your cat grooming tool kit.

Chapter 14: Teaching the Cat Not to Resist Having Nails Clipped.

Cats can induce a lot of harm with their claws, not just to furnishings, however, additionally to the people in their home. In case you have this problem, you may wish to think about having your cat's claws clipped. This is specifically crucial in case you have kids in your house.

Cat clippers are readily offered at most pet stores. Do not utilize the identical clippers on your cat that you might utilize for yourself. These are not to be used on an animal and are going to pinch the claws painfully. It's a great plan to get your kitten accustomed to having its claws managed right from when it is small. Wait up until it is feeling drowsy-- on your lap is a great location to have the cat. Manage its claws and paws often by carefully holding them squeezing them, picking them up and playing lightly with them. In this manner, it is going to see that you mean it no harm when touching its feet. Keep in mind that cats' feet are really delicate and tender.

You are going to have the ability to make the cat unsheathe its claws in case you carefully squeeze its paws. Run your fingers carefully across the claws a number of times, however, in case it attempts to scratch you, merely stop and wait up until it ends up being drowsy once again. It might take numerous days for the kitten to start to accept having its paws and claws touched. It is a good idea to do it frequently, even when its claws do not require clipping, due to the fact that then the cat is going to be so accustomed to it that it is not going to mind.

As soon as you believe the cat is happy to have you have fun with its claws, and it does not attempt to scratch you, you can present the clippers. Once again, wait up until the cat is in a drowsy mood before you begin to clip. It might be a good idea for you to simply hold the cat, while another individual does the clipping. That way, you'll have the ability to protect against any unexpected motions on kitten's part that might lead to injury of the cat or you.

When you are having fun with kitten's claws, take a good look and you'll notice the cloudy, pinkish part close to where the nail comes out of the sheath.

Make certain to never ever clip into this part, or you are going to induce a lot of pain to the kitten, and its claws are going to bleed. If the kitten really does not like to get its nails clipped and yet they need to be, it could be wrapped up in a towel to assist with holding the cat and shielding you from scratching.

Some individuals have their cat's front claws removed. It could be an unpleasant procedure, however, if you have a cat that you simply are unable to teach not to scratch your antique furnishings, this could be what's needed. This procedure ought to just be performed by a vet, and if you follow his or her directions, the preliminary pain is short-lived.

Chapter 15: Teaching Tricks

The very best method to teach your cat tricks is by using its natural behavior. In the zoo, you are going to typically see animals such as a tiger or a lion that leap to their food. In the wilderness, these animals do these things naturally. They are a part of the cat's regular conduct, so this makes training them a lot easier. So, are there any other natural behaviors that cats have?

They enjoy climbing up and leaping, so any trick that entails this is going to be one that cat ought to take to without any problem. For example, you might train it to leap from one stool to another to get the food. Obviously, if the cat then wishes to leap from the stool onto the counter where you do not want it, you may have an issue.

Cats enjoy to chase after and pounce on anything that moves, so if you have a trick where the cat goes after something, ensure it additionally rustles. Small kitties are more vivacious than mature ones, so this is a great time to teach them tricks. Kitties are going to go after a shadow on the floor usually. In case this is your hand's shadow, you could make it go up the wall, and the cat is going to leap after it.

An older cat is going to typically go after a tennis ball which the kids are hitting to one another throughout the backyard, particularly if it bounces. To the cat, it appears like a mouse. This behavior can frequently be integrated into what appears to be some type of trick.

Cats are extremely fast to notice moving things, so you could get your cat to appear like it is shaking its head, simply by utilizing a motion at every side of the room. This could be started up a bit closer, then slowly moved further away. A noise might be utilized initially to make the cat to look a certain way.

When training your cat tricks, do not perplex it by attempting to do a number of them at the same time. Utilize one motion or technique at a time and stop as quickly as the cat loses interest. Select the time of day when that cat appears to be most lively in order to encourage these lively behaviors, and the cat is going to quickly come to anticipate them eagerly. Soon, you'll have

it doing tricks, and it'll believe it's the very best fun it has ever had. Do not forget to award the cat whenever it does anything you desire, and don't forget to be patient. Never penalize the cat if it does not do what you desire.

I hope that you enjoyed reading through this book and that you have found it useful. If you want to share your thoughts on this book, you can do so by leaving a review on the Amazon page. Have a great rest of the day.

Printed in Great Britain
by Amazon

15053054R00031